# CURSED TO FEEL

## CHELSEA LITTLE

GUILDFORD • 2019

# CURSED TO FEEL

## CHELSEA LITTLE

GUILDFORD · 2019

ABOUT THE AUTHOR

# CHELSEA LITTLE

Chelsea grew up in Stourbridge, West Midlands, UK. Although focusing on academics when she was younger she studied a three year BA HONS degree at PPA drama school to pursue her passion of musical theatre.

Although the theatre has her heart, creativity is in her veins and poetry and song writing has always been an outlet for Chelsea in times of extreme emotion. She writes from the soul and her ultimate goal is create and produce content that resonates with others to build a community of self love and positivity! You do you!

Follow her on Instagram @chelseaisalittle and @smiletohealth for more content

ABOUT THE ILLUSTRATOR

# SOPHIA NICOLELLA

Sophia grew up and currently resides in Ridgefield, Connecticut, USA. She studied Fine Arts at the University of Connecticut and received her BFA with a concentration in illustration and stop-motion animation.

Although her full time job is a graphic designer for a market research company, Sophia still finds time to freelance illustrations, paintings, and logos. She enjoys experimenting with reality and the make-believe, using imagery inspired by forests and fairytales to build her own world in each piece of art.

You can find more of her work at:
*https://www.behance.net/sophianicolella*

*For those that think too much, feel too much, and simply need to just be.*

# Contents

# Love

The balance of pain and passion

**Always**

It's you I'm gonna miss
because I thought you could fix
me but you left me broken again
left me broken in pain
with just a kiss.
I don't care if you're not my forever
just be my right now
me. You. Together
It'll work somehow.

It's you
all of you
that makes sense
in this world of pretence
where I can only see in monochrome
In my search of a home in technicolour
that is you my lover.
The rainbow, a work of art
that stabs my heart with every rejection
in my need for connection
I disconnect with myself
become someone else
in hope that that someone will be
something you crave.

It's you I want to misbehave for

take the leap
yearn for more
love. Want. Trust.
I need this to be more than lust
because our souls are tied
and I have cried
too much already
this woman of fire can't go steady
when she burns aflame
and you're to blame
for setting her alight
and making her want to fight
for a world and a feeling bigger than herself
than a world that has been nothing else
but cruel.

From relationships to school
she's had no luck
got stuck
with pain, struggle and a constant uphill
so don't add to the bill of sadness
treat her like a goddess
like you did at the start
a work of art
you said
well pick up the paint brush
there's no rush

let's start again.
It's you. Always you.

## Strong woman

I can't escape or run away
from the things you did
or used to say.
It's a funny thing - aha 'funny' you said
but where's the laughter
you left me dead

inside. I felt broken, lost, alone.
I couldn't leave the house
or even check my phone.
You wounded me, in the worst way how
by tossing me aside and cheating with that

cow. Pardon me
excuse my language
I'm not very good at associating with
garbage.
You think I'm weak
nothing without you
but I'm standing tall
and doing things you'll never do.

Oh look. Hey boo!
How's your life?
When you still live at home
praying for a country wife.

I'm living it up in the cityscape of
London town
with confidence as my mother f*cking gown.

You blocked me. You abused me
with words so full of hate,
sent me letters and painted me green
but I wouldn't reciprocate

to your silly little games
with your beard as pathetic as your plan
to ruin me and make me grovel
well sorry - I don't need a man.

## Notification

Just a call. A text.
Just a tag in a photo
or a funny request.
Funny.
You used to be funny.

I would say *do you remember that time?*
But you blocked me
haha from your timeline.
So now I'm lost in the data
the numbers
the lines
of a different photo and another time.

Time.
It's just a part of your imagination
a  fearful  clock  to  calculate  our
destination.
But it makes us stop. What?
Where did the time go?
I thought you cared
I didn't want you to go.

You left. Bam. Just like that
there was no going back.
You wouldn't listen
couldn't hack it

when things got tough.
I thought you were better than that
wasn't I enough?

**Fine**

Smile.
Because everything is fine,
I'm fine. I'm good
at being fine.

But I'm not fine.
Fine was lost in your head games
your head fucks
your 'let's just be friends'
your lies
your deceit
your godforsaken smile.
That smile.

Those texts you never replied too
those tears you never responded too
those days you were supposed to remember.
But you never remembered.

Funny thing is I'm fine.
I learnt how to be fine.
I kept telling myself I'm fine.
Now without you
I'm fine.

## Full stop

You're just a bump in the road
a blip, a mistake
that has no power
or control over my fate.
Yet I can't help but wonder why
did you enter my life
when you knew I wasn't right
right for you? No that isn't the word
I can't believe I'm writing this
the whole thing seems so absurd.

Breakup.

The word itself is an oxymoron
sat together, not separated
or relevant to what a relationship can
become.
All or nothing
that's what it is
a journey of extremes
their memory nothing more than a dream.
Are we meant to learn
to discover something about who we are?
Because my head is a mess
due to the journey so far.

I can still feel the burn

of the end, the full stop.
The book has been closed
on a love I never expected
a love I never expected to lose.
To stop.

## Etiquette

We are born alone
and told to find our own way.
Yet we are conditioned to believe
there must come a day
where you build a life no longer for
yourself
your own selfish needs must rest upon a
shelf.

Tie the knot
do things the proper way
find yourself a man
and make sure you stay
faithful, beautiful and as pleasing as you
can
it wasn't what you wanted
but you better stick to the plan.

Single? Oh that's such a shame
you shouldn't be so frigid
weren't you taught to play the game?
Dress up, dumb down
masquerade a caricature
of a *you* society approves of
that guarantees allure.

Comfort, yes a comfortable life

is what you must achieve as your role of a wife.
A ring on your finger and a baby on the way
you can't remember the last time you used to play.

Play, have fun and simply be you
every day was an adventure
a chance to see something new.

Don't let the world
convince you to change
to suppress your inner child and rearrange
the very fibres of your being
the fibres within you that make your inner child sing.

## Mr/Mrs right

Inhale. Exhale. Repeat.
Out the badness of the world
all the lies and deceit.
Where's true love in this world? Is it all
just a fleet-
ing memory, a fairytale, a once upon a
time
when people weren't afraid to feel
and put themselves on the line.
Line, a journey but we aren't moving very
fast
we're stuck-
stood still, all too hooked upon our past.
Letting it define us, trick us into making
the same mistakes
so blinded that the beauty of today
we never appreciate.
Until it's too late
BOOM- time has begun to dissipate
so we wonder what could have been
if we'd only took the time to wait.
For the right one
not right now.

## That thing we call dating

You can never really lose
or permanently erase
someone from your life
as much as we delete and try to forget
memories can't disappear with a single
swipe.

Left. Right. Super like
everyone is at your fingertips
commitment is now a foreign concept
anyone is at your lips.

Easy, short term, one night stand
terms that used to remain
for celebs in a band
the groupies, the people that had no care
in the world
but I do care and is a relationship too
much for a girl

to ask for, to want, to need or desire?
If you don't sleep around you're frigid
but if you do it ignites a fire
of hate and judgement from people
that do the same
society is so shallow
their views all so lame.

Broaden your mind
and see the bigger picture
life is so much more
than a temporary fixture.

Stand up be different
don't log up the exes
throw away your tally chart
and appreciate the sexes.

## It's a fine line

It amazes me really
how childish you can be
with that cheeky smile and voice like
velvet
you think you can achieve everything.
Indestructible champion of all champs
with everyone and everything at your feet
well I'm not property mr
so don't treat me like I'm cheap-

A possession, just another one of your
toys
get your head out your arse
and run back to the boys.
Tell stories, play games like you always
do
but don't come running to me
when your dummy falls askew.

You lost the bet and failed to see
beyond the ego you've made into
a forcefield of charm and flair
when desperately all you want
is someone to care.
Well I cared and I cried enough about you
so bye-bye baby cakes try not to look so
blue.

Now I'm empowered and strong
a woman rising above your dolls
so look at me and take a good look
because what you said about me—
well WOW you were wrong.

## Fame

It's like being in a prison
except you have freedom to talk
to walk around as you please
within a certain division.
But your oxygen is monitored
one switch bam you're suffocated
gasping for air
and the worse thing is that nobody cares.
You're trapped within this illusion of
everything being fine
but every day, every 8am
is another walk on the line.
A decision and determination to try and
make it through
when in reality your heart is sobbing
and you don't know what to do
but you smile and wave and
like always act strong.
So despite the inner turmoil no one knows
what's wrong.

## Discovery

It's like you came out of nowhere
an unexpected song
that's complicated rhythms drew me in
made me smile
a smile of warmth and truth
the kind that caresses your whole body
in a protective embrace
that creates strength but also release
as you feel like you can finally breathe
again
as though I'm finally home.

## Truth

Emptiness.
That's the true dagger in everyone's
souls.
Not sadness, loneliness or desperation
as that black hole embodies
all of the above.
A void.
We frantically attempt to fill
stuff, starve, buy
self medicate the self loathing
searching for a home and human connection.
But we're disconnected
a life behind a screen instead of in the
moment
short term love in short term flings
rather than long term self care.
Care? Rules, terms and conditions
in a merry go round of obligations
going nowhere but still catapulting us
further from ourselves.
Our truth.

## True love

I'm not scared to feel
to remember the warmth of love in my soul
and pressure of fingers on my skin
or the running of tears down my cheeks
washing away the memories
of all the pain that's been.

My fear is not to feel or express
passion, love and all the chaos
in between.
My fear is spending so long feeling
nothing at all
you never truly feel it again.
True love.

# Mind

The home we forget to take
care of

## Lbs

She stands
and stares
a look that is all too long and familiar.
One that brands
and glares
at every flaw reflected back at her.

Beauty.
A construct that seems so out of reach
Ugly.
Well at least you can always bleach
and blot and brush away
the flaws that mark you wrong.
Lose some weight
pout those lips
and for goodness sake know where you
belong.

Lbs and pounds
endless numbers that form a chart
of the worthy and the admirable
you're either trash or a work of art.
Names, places, brands
all temporary ticks on a list
yet nobody seems to understand
that time is the one that ticks.

Tick tock
goes the continuous hand of time
as your numbers start to drop
with every snort of a line.
Further and further we are digging our own
graves
yet everyone is trapped in this mind set
the world cannot be saved.

The world has become a cruel
unforgiving place
most girls now have the faded stream
of tears running down their face.
Due to shame, frustration and pure
self hate
that society has broken them
and left them with one cruel fate.

Thin.

**Thin**

It starts with something small
like a comment or a phase
that made me stop and think
that myself, me, I, should be rearranged.

"You're not as pretty as that girl
why can't you look more like her?"
"You need to lose weight you're eating too
much"
the happy days became a blur.
As I counted and catapulted
into a self destruction spiral
but everyone applauded me
the new *me* went viral.

My parents started to notice
I became popular at school
I was starving and felt so empty
but seemed like skinny is deemed as cool.

Cool like my body
my fingers and my feet
but I can't remember when I saw my friends
my life is exercise, starve repeat.
The weight keeps dropping on the scale
but I'm declared beautiful in dance

maybe if I just keep pushing forward
someone will give me a chance?
To be me and show me
to the people that actually want to see
I have so much to offer
please let me make ME happy.
I'm tired, I'm hurting and I feel so alone
this used to make me feel powerful
but now I just want somewhere
to feel like home.

Not a torture chamber, trap or cave
to get the love I need too breathe
but you let me dig my grave
now a future - I no longer see.

## Perception

Semi's and demi's
halves and extra small
too little is just right
but too much and you lose it all.
Inches
Lbs
Worth in numbers
figures, facts it's all just a bundle of
bull-
shocking actually what is said, what is
believed
conditioned to hate and doubt our
self worth
from the moment we're conceived.
Conception, perception we all have eyes
yet we close them
dispose of our power
to change and control how we feel
we have no independence
we're all hamsters on a wheel.
Running, lifting, hashtag 'fitspoing' our
lives away
all because of that day
you believed
you accepted
a story you didn't write
about who you are

a person filled with fright.
Towards that little piece of glass that
turns you so pale
your reflection in the mirror
a number on the scale.

## Struggles

Through the grim and the struggles
I've come to know
that life isn't about getting everything
just so
perfect, to a t, whatever you want to call
it
life is more than a filing system
of certificates, medals and applause.
It's about finding those sweet moments
that you'd relive without a pause
hesitation, anxiety and doubting
your self worth
all because of some system that's f-
designed to make you hurt.
Well my wounds are healing
and I'm beginning to create a shield
of my own love and aspirations
that will guide me through the field
of challenges, self doubt and world wide
critique
I'm following my heart and don't need to
compete
with the structure, the pressures and
rules of how to live a life
I'm done with destruction
I'm filled with love
so I'm handing back the knife.

## Wounded

There are wounds that never appear on the
body
that hurt more than anything that bleeds
sometimes we want to be loved so badly
we can't even recognise our needs
beyond the people pleasing, social
acceptance
and just trying to get by
we focus too much on the goals
and not enough on the why.

If the wounds on people's hearts
and the bruises on their souls
were translated onto their skin
we'd have a map of self destruction
marking the journey we have been
on and are still progressing through
the highs and lows teaching us something
new.
A learning curve like a smile or the sun
life is heavy but we've only just begun.

Being alone will scare you
but not accepting help will scar you
shame needs to be knocked out
of the equation

truth and reality broadcasted on every
station
raw, uncomfortable and everything the
world should know
because mental illness is a battlefield
not a glamorised show.

## Shine

It's gonna get harder
before it gets better
the tears will run rivers down the roses
of your cheeks
before the glisten of a smile returns.
But nothing beautiful was created through comfort
and from the sand a diamond shall form
and you will shine.
Your beauty. Your happiness. Yourself.

## Yoga

Life is a balance of holding on
and letting go.
Self care is reminding ourselves
that we already know
what to do, eat, feel and say
life is knowing that no matter what
you'll always find your way.

## Wild

I want to feel so alive
that I'm wild like the ocean
crashing down onto the ground
ethereal like the clouds
wise observers without a sound
strong like the sun
the goddess of them all
grounded like the roots of a tree
refusing not to stand tall.
But most of all
I want to feel like the moon
new sides appearing all the time
throwing tides just for fun
creating because it's all I am
and all I want to become.

## Habits

I look in the mirror and I'm sick of
hating what I see
I just want an ounce of happy
or love or SOMETHING
other than this empty void of nothing.
No words, just suffocation
it's like I am stuck on a station of white
noise
no voice to articulate the pain I feel
knowing that I am stuck on a hamster wheel
of self destruct vs self love.
trying to make a life I am proud of
whilst that god damn mirror just shows me
the truth.

Youth has not been my friend
as my mental health goes down a bend
in the road and I get hit. Hard.
My guards are up and my serotonin is low
I don't understand where to go from here
on a path I know all too well
I stood then I fell
into the same old well of hate
my weight
dictating my life
and I've had enough!

I don't want to be tough
and fight when I don't know what I'm
fighting for
every time I try to open a door
of opportunity rejection
hits me in the face
weight gain has taken weight losses place
and that face
is fuller
but duller
struggling with the diagnosis of healthy
and well
when the reality is I'm living a hell
that far surpasses the struggle of skinny.
It's the struggle of me.

My mind and the attempt to find freedom
in a metaphorical kingdom which I'm held
prisoner but convinced I'm free
in the comfort zone of happy
that's in fact bad habits on repeat
I've just about admitted defeat
this is beyond the simple act of eat-
ing for fuel, health, recovery, whatever
all I know is that I don't want this to be
my forever
I want to live not exist.
But I'm tired of having to persist

through the drudge of my own brain
that is ignited with pain
and in desperate need of breath
an election
of a healthy end to a spectrum
and human connection
love.
Something I can only ever dream of.

# You

Forgotten but your forever
friend

## Sagittarius woman

She was in love with the world in a way
she could never be in love with here
filling up her cups
on the horizons of the clear
and unclear paths of her future and
undetermined plans.
Unmanned, unpredictable
a fireball of curiosity
possibility
at her fingertips
her heart longing for the beauty of the
world
her duty sworn to the god of wanderlust
thrusting her onto a path of the unknown
and she has flown
to the edge of danger and dare
without a care
and she'll continue to fly
and defy
expectations thrust upon her.
For she's the perfect blend of
fire and water
she is freedoms daughter
a goddess of the sun and the moon
a flower in bloom
a sagittarius woman.

## Honey

Oh honey
don't stress that you don't have it all
figured out
you're like a tree shredding it's leaves
changing colour, growing.
Constantly.

Oh honey,
smile and be you
be in the now
yes be the beauty of the moment
and the transparency of yourself.

Oh honey
you are surrounded by inspiration,
potential and love
don't you ever forget your worth.

Oh honey
take a picture, write stuff down,
create, create, create
Oh honey
you know what?
You're doing great.

## Self love club

There are many people who would
say, comment or claim to understand
the aching pain in your heart
that takes over your brain
makes you do things you never planned
would happen or not happen as the case may
be
life used to be so easy.
Fun you could say
when you didn't have to live day by day
praying you'll find that ache in your
heart
and fill it with love
a love you were born with
but educated to forget
A love that meant so much more than
the meaningless alphabet
That feeling that you are enough.

## Equilibrium

A life of extremes
so many boundaries
yet completely limitless.
Balance.
A simple word
2 syllables in fact
but too many meanings to understand
to feel understood
to reenact, live and play
a part
whilst remaining true to the person she
was at the start.
Balance.

## Learning

She smiled
a smile that went so deeply
the drum of her heartbeat
radiated the love within her soul.
The love she was finally learning
to have
to save
to give
to herself.

## Mystery

Her eyes were a whirlpool of mystery
the blues and greens enveloping one
another
in a tangled mess of love and despair.
Perfect.
Perfectly imperfect
is the longing to understand
her tortured soul behind her eyes
within her gypsy spirit.

## Rays

Smile my dear
smile and shine so brightly
that all the darkness that tried to
overcome you
will hide in the shadows
because you are light.
You are love
and you are enough.
So smile honey
because it's what you do best.

## Rise

She tore out the paper
and burnt the stories others had written.
For she was the author of her own life
a free spirit, a warrior,
who would rise from the ashes
only to glow brighter than she had before.

## Self Love

So she kept searching
only to be hurt and disappointed
because she sort an answer in wanderlust
when the answer was in herself.

## Enough

As my mind unlocked the chains
bound by self doubt and neglect
fuelled by hatred
my body sighed with relief
as the wind was allowed to rest
the internal monologue released.
An exhale of freedom
from the catalogue of destructive thoughts
paving way, opening up space
for love and forgiveness.
And the words I'd been longing to hear
but could never find.
You are enough.

## Worth

I know my worth
I've spent most of my life
explaining
justifying
defending
a fact of nature that doesn't need a
defence
My worth.
My opinions.
My identity.
The truth.

## Gypsy soul

To travel is to find yourself
in places you never knew you'd find
to broaden the mind
and indulge in cultures and friendships
you'll never forget.
Time is never a concept
there's no boundaries of 9-5
you create and build the foundations of
your own life
missing the home you used to call base
and the calm you find in every other place
of your adventures.

Seeing the world from the opposite side of
the moon
seeing yourself in an alternative lifetime
the big wide world that seems so small.
Travelling is extending the conversation
and shortening the to do list
letting go of the existential crisis and
just existing.

Travel.

It's not just about planting your feet
in the sands of the globe
and bearing the memories on your back.

It's about connecting back to who you
truly are
but opening doors for the person you want
to be
but society told you to forget.

## Musings

I love this life
this web of lessons
that help me fall more in love
with everything this world has to offer
everything I have to offer.
And as the ocean washes away the sand
I feel reborn
like a warrior on a mission
to prove to herself
what the world told her she can't be
but always knew she could.

# Short

## Pockets of thought

## Damaged goods

I'm scared, I'm broken
I've been tested and confused.
My mind is overwhelmed
by the world that has bruised-
me and taken me to the darkest of places.
But light appears in the form of new faces
friends
and faith in what I have done.
I've been through hell and back
but the BEST is yet to come.

## Healing

It's ok to admit
that you haven't healed
are still figuring it out
finding *you* in the cracks and
gaps between the seams.
Seams, sizes it's all a load of bull-
sit down, calm down
you're more than what you think.
Eat the burger live your life
don't throw it away down the sink.
Keep your hands out your throat
and your head held high
start living for the yes
not stressing over the why
the how and the what was that for?
Honey you're a fighter and it's about time
you knew
what you were fighting for.
You. Yourself. That's enough.

## Self

I'm tired of measuring my self worth
on the thickness of my thighs
judging my potential on my level of lows
rather than the beauty of the highs.
High, self medicating, self loathing
all the selfies but no true…self.

**Wanderlust**

Some think I'm lost
and maybe that's true
as my soul is in love
with what the world can do.

## Games

It's not white or black
no jackpot to be won
because the reality is
love is a cruel game that
so many don't realise they've begun.

**Listen**

Listening.
The true skill that provides
answer and understanding
without uttering a word.

**Reflection**

Mirror.
Once we see the reflective object for
what it is
an object
we shall start acknowledging it's
falseness
in deciding our worth.

**Modern relationships**

There's nothing like the pain
of having lost
something you never really had.

**Storm**

When the sky screams out thunderstorms
it's anger illuminating the sky
she is reminded that even the heavens
can lose control.
But it's in this loss
that you find yourself in the stars.

## Craving

It's hard not to fall
into the tomb of loneliness.
The darkness of reminiscing what it is to
be craved
to be appreciated
to be loved.

## Oxymoron

She is a living oxymoron
the bittersweet
blend of day and night
a smile masking an inner sadness
and complicated soul.
A beauty beyond a good contour
a thrilling fusion of both the beginning
and the end.

## Piece by piece

The prize is in the process
in the pieces
you think are broken
impossible to put back together
where your inner peace is found.
Piece by piece.

## Space

You should never apologise for taking time
for yourself
for setting aside the to do lists
the commitments
the people to see
to find some time out and space to just
breathe.
To focus on your hobbies, your dreams and
bigger plans
or to just take a moment
and know your life doesn't have to be
manned
by the clock
the expectations
and pressures of the world.
This world, the earth what a place
we only get one chance
so don't be scared to fill up your space.

**Goddess**

Own your body
wear it with pride
love every curve
and stripe along the way
because honey you're beautiful
and don't let anyone tell you otherwise.

## Test

I guess it's a test
I feel like I've been hexed
but it's just sex
human connection
but on reflection
I know I should have been safe.
Saved.
Is the child I decide to say no
let it go
to let myself live.
I'm not asking for forgive-
ness or to be accepted
for the baby I rejected
when I know it's the right choice.
It's my body
my voice.

# Spoken Word
## Loud and proud

## Twenty something

Spending another day in front of my fear
staring myself in the eyes
wishing I could just disappear
to a place where I was safe, happy, secure
and knew what the f*ck all this constant
struggle was for.
Surrounded by rejection
comparison a drug
with no connection
my life being a constant string of never
as I struggle in the turmoil to find my
forever
when I'm not even half way through my day
yet
through my years yet.
I'm not even 25
and I'm made to feel I've failed in this
life
but I've never felt more alive
despite not having anyone by my side
because I'm ok. In this life
figuring out ME rather than the role of
a wife
a career or whatever we're taught to be
all of the labels that are far from happy.
Too much time spent on everyone else

yet so little time to find ourself
in this catastrophe of looks, likes and
retweets
self doubt ingrained before we learn to
stand on our own two feet.
You can't heal by going back to the thing
that broke you
yet you can be broken without a need to
transform into something new
to see the beauty in the imperfection
rather than scrutinising under close
inspection
every unique thing about yourself
that marks who you are and offers the
world something else
so amazing, electrifying and beyond the
scars
of the battle you've fought through so far
it's ok
stop.
Have you ever taken a moment to see what
you've got?
The right here, right now see the glass
half full
hashtag namaste all that yogi bull
I've done the gap yah I'm a walking cliche
I ran away from Oxford and jumped on a
plane

because the 'normal' life was driving me
insane
I needed a bit of me again
wow that rhyming is getting a bit lame
but you get what I mean, laugh away
laugh, fill your body with the love of
today
because it's far to easy to sit in what we
know
when we have the power to let it all go
break out of the cry, abuse, repeat
a constant defeat
in the carbon copy life we are programmed
to seek
nothing
coming of it when all we want is enough.
To breathe
to be
the unique gem of our individuality
that is manipulated into sin
when what we've always been
is enough.

## Happiness

She's the happiest in the room
a smile spread across her face
hanging a curtain over the years
of tears cascading down her cheeks
she's in everyone's phone book
and on the end of everyones speech
but no one takes the time to check on her
week
her day
say, how are you babe?
Check that behind that show reel
everything's ok
because it's easy to be the sunshine
the ray of light
but the hard bit is acknowledging
that sometimes everything isn't alright
life is hard, tough and a road out of
balance
every time you step up you're thrown
another challenge
that we think we have to do alone
our biggest fear now being on our own
rather than being the better
half of ourself
not looking for fulfilment in someone else
or something else

a career, a car, a holiday
something to mask away
the reality of the day
the week or the year you've had
which seems bad
when actually there's been so much good
we've just been trapped in this
misunderstood
concept that success is only tangible on
an insta worthy scale
of money, likes and an edited greyscale
of that highlight reel we believe is life
when that's just the tip of the knife
barricading the beauty of the journey
the progress of learning
from every mistake, trip and fall along
the way
that finally leads to the day
where you can proudly say
happiness
well that's enough.

## Whole

Is this what it's like
to be out one night
and be so blissfully unaware
of everyone else in sight
apart from what's right in front of you.
I mean this is all very new
I've always been shut off
show people the chapters I want them to
see
trapped in my own deluded concept of happy
that kept me smiling but secluded from
real connection
due to my own perception
that putting myself on the line meant I
was weak
was admitting defeat
to the cliche of once upon a time
I didn't want to be a princess story line
so I took the pen and wrote my own novel
I wasn't gonna sit and grovel
over a happy ever after that never reached
the ball
the point where people have it all
or whatever it's meant to be
just didn't seem like me
but you see

in my desperate attempt to run away from
love
I stumbled into the arms of
a person I never imagined would make me
smile
stop
and think about something else for a while
and break down my wall
bit by bit
not one big hit
but a gradual thaw
of the heart I thought was stone
as I got to know
and feel more at home
with a guy that understood my scars
and healed my wounds
respected my bars
and didn't push me to swoon
I just fell.
Hard. Into his smile, laugh and beating
heart
his stories a work of art
he held up a mirror to myself
highlighting how in putting myself on the
shelf
I'd become a forgotten story
an allegory

a cliche of women who cut themselves off
from love
because they couldn't even dream of
the beauty it brings
instead I made a list of things
that made me not good enough
a shield of tough
because I didn't need a man
unaware that you can
want someone without needing them
and that beautiful things can happen
when you know it's what you deserve
and that what you seek is not to serve
another but to feel safe
every time you see them you escape
from all the hardship you face on your own
and return to a home
where you can be yourself
whilst completing someone else
well you know what I'm ready
for the heavy
the romance
to take a chance
on something beyond my control
if there's even the slightest chance I can
feel whole
again.

## Broken

Did you know that
I loved you from the start
did you know that
I was never playing a part
or that piece by piece as you built me up
from the ground
I thought for the first time maybe
I'm ready to be found
to be part of the chaos that is romance
little miss single was ready to give love
a chance
and you loved me
well I thought you did
seemed happy
but then I guess you can never know what's
in someone else's head.
Did you know that
you were never gonna stay
did you know that
you'd just walk away
and leave me standing there
thinking you cared
and blaming myself for the destruction
creating an endless construction
of lists of why I'm not good enough
worthy of happiness or feeling like home

with someone rather than lost and alone
but then I'm used to that
aren't I?
I never hid the fact
that I have cried
before and loved and been so hurt
but it wasn't my story you cared about
I was a pawn in your plan to figure things
out
well I hope the dots align
and that you're feeling just fine
because actually I'm not
and I had forgot
what it was like to let someone in
to comprehend the fact it was possible to
begin
again
but now my walls are up higher than before
as I wonder what the hell this whole love
thing is for
because I'm damaged
every time I open up more baggage
that I can't carry anymore
I'm  falling to the floor
under the weight of this world that isn't
my friend
and to be honest I just want it to end
because I always try to do the right thing

but nothing good happens in return
maybe I was evil in a past life
but I think I've had my fair share of
having to learn
call me Icarus I'm aflame
flown too close to the sun
and I know there's no one to blame
but I'm going insane
and my life has barely begun.
What did I do that was so wrong
to perpetually feel like I don't belong
the pen is down I've drawn the end
full stop.
I'm done with having to pretend
I'm happy with what I've got
when I am but with no one to share it with
makes me wonder where the care is
but I guess that's just life
balancing on the blade of a knife
waiting
to take that leap of faith
change of pace
and after falling for so long eventually
you get caught
by a soul that was everything you thought
you never deserved
but was waiting there all along
I just pray I'm not wrong.

## You

You leaving was like being evicted from a
house
that was never truly home
just bricks and stone
an empty shell
representing the hell
I'm now feeling
show reeling
in my head
all the best moments I never foretold
punishing myself with things I should have
said
I just want you to hold
me again.
You repeat your same explanations
that don't offer any conclusion
just trap me in a delusion
that I was more than a game
on your playstation
a notch on your tally chart
but to become what we are now
was it ever real at the start?
Because I stand by what I said
you were never misled
I cared and do care about you
and every inch of your life

I wasn't looking for something new
or to be your future wife
I just wanted you
all that you are
I relished every scar
and achievement so far
but for you it wasn't enough
maybe the grass was greener
or things got tough?
But I was a believer in this world you
fabricated
your behaviour outdated but divine
a gentlemen on the front line
fighting for his country as well as
himself
and for me or so I believed
not after satisfaction or wealth
or was I deceived
and you're just another one of those guys
that brings tears to women's eyes
as we try to think what the f*ck went
wrong
why we can't play our song
or think about that time on New Years Eve
where I actually believed
this was SOMETHING
not just a someone
but a hope and love to depend upon

when those days did get rough
and I wasn't enough
because you know all about that
but still you hurt me with that swing of a
bat
of a line so overdone
well you've won
happy now, have you got what you wanted
because now my mind is haunted
by all the bad things I make myself think
true
about me not you
yes I'm damaged too
but I guess you couldn't see that far
could you?

## Home

There's something about going home
returning to the place where it all began
knowing that the beginning
is where the sense of belonging
was all along.
And life seems long
and broken
disjointed
in places that were supposed to make sense
in this world of pretence
where success equals happiness
surrounded by a fence of
a new city, a big place
somewhere to fill up space
but you're in fact squeezing into crevices
trying to find the premises
of the purpose in all this.
As the lines appear on your face
and the work piles on your desk
you realise that home isn't a place
but a person. People.
That there's beauty in the rest
rather than the repeated schedule
constantly trying to get ahead
but getting nowhere.
Maybe that's why it's called a timeline

because we're walking the plank looking
for a lifeline
one direction and one ending
that we're all pretending we have
  control of
when in fact we're merely a product of
society.
Of the lie we all believe
from the day we're conceived
but then told to forget
that we actually have a say in what lies
ahead
and you can step back as well as forwards
create a path of all direction
be an exception
to all the rules
and be the ruler of your own life.
Hold the pen and take a strike
against convention and consistency
be who YOU want to be
not what you're told to desire
reignite that fire
that burns so bright but you suppress away
simmer down with fake happiness
like a short holiday, pay rise
or a swanky new car
when actually you aren't happy with life
so far

but that's ok
today is a new day
and so is tomorrow.
So let go of what is or should be
and embrace the possibility
of YOUR life.
Yes it's yours
so go get it.
Be a rebel without a cause.

# Acknowledgements

Initially I was going to write a list of names of all the people I wanted to thank, but there are so many inspirational souls I've met in my life that have kept me on the path to pursuing all things creativity, I'm going to leave them anonymous. You know who you are, and you're fabulous! Apart from my family, who have funded the very expensive career of being creative…here's your special mention.

*xoxo*
*C*

# CURSED TO FEEL

## CHELSEA LITTLE

GUILDFORD • 2019

Printed in Great Britain
by Amazon

32961431R00054